Sensei Diane,

Thank you for teaching me that I Am, "10ft Tall and bulletproof." You impacted my life & journey deeply!

Subira Folami

How to Transform Wounds to Wisdom and Create a New Life!

By Subira Folami

How to Transform Wounds to Wisdom and Create a New Life

Mail to:

Attn: Subira Folami

9613C Harford Rd #199

Baltimore, MD 21234

Website http://www.SenseiSubira.com/VIP
Facebook: Sensei Subira
Periscope: @SenseiSubira
IG: @SenseiSubira

Email:subira.folami@gmail.com

Contact number:434-8-SUBIRA 434-878-2472

Bulk Ordering Information:

Special discounts are available on quantity purchases by corporations, associations, and others. For details, contact the publisher at the address above.

Orders by U.S trade bookstores and wholesalers contact the office of Subira Media at the contact information above.

Table of Contents

About this Book

"Sit at the feet of your own life and learn from it."
~Sensei Subira

Perhaps you are a massage therapist, a spiritual teacher, community leader, an energy healer, an artist or a yoga practitioner. Major life changes like illness, loss of employment, divorce, geographic relocation, or even the death of a loved one can devastate and completely disrupt your life.

After living through a major life change, you have come to a place of absolute clarity that you have not been living in alignment with the patterns, the blueprint and the purpose of your life. You realize that you can no longer fit into a 9-to-5 job setting.

This book, *How to Transform Wounds to Wisdom and Create a New Life!* serves to give you, the person who lives your life in service to others, a curriculum for the studies of transformation.

After your life has been completely turned upside down, *How to Transform Wounds to Wisdom and Create a New Life!* offers a roadmap to support you in finding your way to your "new normal." The book teaches you to how to be your *own* hero or Sacred Warrior by showing you how to look inside yourself and harness the wisdom you've learned during your time on your transformational journey.

Through one or more life-altering experiences, you have been gifted with the vision outlining why you are on the planet. However, you may still feel that you cannot sustain yourself with your innate gifts.

Your Story Has Value

I wrote this book as an offering to the contrary. Not only can you create a healthy living from the stories and gifts of your life's journey, but that is one of the major reasons that you had the life-transforming experience in the first place.

The fact that you did live to tell your story means that you conquered the challenges placed in front of you. You demonstrated self-mastery as you came to understand the lessons that presented themselves as you moved farther along your path.

The tables have now turned and what was once "your" story becomes the self-mastery you developed that allows you to share the lessons, insights and wisdom from a place of power rather than a place of victimhood. The story is obliged to serve you and those who support you as you learn to close the door on ways of BEing, thinking, and even behaving that no longer serve you.

The process you lived through has transformed you and brought you into a new awareness of yourself, your purpose and the world around you. You suddenly get it! The life you were living *had to be completely destroyed* so that you would re-create a life that is in alignment with the gifts, insights and wisdom gained while you were being transformed during your Hero's Journey.

How to Transform Wounds to Wisdom and Create a New Life! explains why it is noble, honorable and responsible to be a spiritual entrepreneur. A spiritual entrepreneur is one who is enlightened and makes mindful moves using spiritual and Internet technology to offer value to a segment of the marketplace that he has made a sacred agreement to serve.

Creating a New Life

From childhood you were taught that you have to work hard, get a "good" 9-to-5 job and work until you are at least 65 years old. The reality is, that model no longer works and for people like you and me--

empaths, lightworkers, indigos--we never fit into that mold.

We are the shapeshifters of the world. We adapted, but for many of us, making these kinds of fundamental adaptations has been slowly sucking the vibrancy of life from us. You believed that this was what you needed to do to survive, so you went along to get along.

Due to the doors that the Internet has opened and the affordability and ease of use of the latest software on the market, that is no longer necessary. Do not allow yourself to grow insensitive to the divine discontent to which you have become accustomed. Do not delay offering the marketplace your gifts.

How to Use This Book

Each chapter of this book covers one of 12 principles of the Sacred Warrior (adapted from Charles Fillmore's *12 Powers of Man*), a lesson based on medicine and a principle. As a martial artist and Budokon yoga practitioner, I could only move from one belt to the next when I displayed proficiency at each level. I thought it would be helpful to assign a belt to each section to represent your increasing mastery as you move through the book.

This book reveals a path that will support you as you move steadily forward on your journey toward discovering the truth of who you are and bolstering you as you make your inner vision congruent with our external world.

This is a multi-faceted process that offers you a way to re~create your life based upon your authentic vision and voice. At its core, this process is about transformation, expansion and transparency for light workers and visionaries from all walks of life.

It is for you who feel called to manifest a healthy living sourced from the lessons, insights, wisdom and medicine that is held deep within the stories of your bones, blood and muscles that you know are being called out in service and leadership to the world.

And if you have not embraced it up to this point, while on the Hero's Journey, the door will open for you. It is then you will learn to express, transform and demonstrate the art of expansive living aligned with the highest version of the most authentic vision for your life at this time.

This book is patterned after "The Hero's Journey," which is described in Joseph Campbell's book, *The*

Hero with a Thousand Faces. In this book, I'll help you to navigate the different states of consciousness that you, the Sacred Warrior and Hero, must live through as you go on this journey of personal development and transformation.

As you begin to correlate your life's journey with that of the Hero's Journey, a sense of freedom will rise up in you, even if you are not yet completely on the other side of the transformation. You will learn to serve from the reserves of your energetic overflow rather than from fear, lack and limitation.

The first and most important thing to understand is that you are embarking upon a process, a Hero's Journey that will transform and expand first you, then your world.

You will experience life as two persons with regard to serving the marketplace: the Hero and the Mentor. This is about you learning a process through which you can share your story of healing transparently and this process will support, sustain and prosper you.

And guess what, your prosperity will prosper an entire community and their prosperity prospers you! Why? Because prosperity is an attractive principle that pulls *toward* the value creator (YOU) every resource you require in order to be fully supported. To the extent that your energy is proven to be a resource for your tribe, prosperity will support you.

Throughout your lifetime, you will cycle and sometimes recycle through your own Hero's Journey story. The key to moving through transformation with ease, elegance and grace is to be able to re~cognize *who* you are in the story, where you are in the story and to consciously choose your mindset as your story progresses. This allows you to be intentional about how you will move through the story knowing you are creating with every choice and every movement.

The Hero and Sacred Warrior

There are many different manifestations of the Hero, and in this process, we will be learning about the Transcendent Hero, the hero of tragedy, who must deal with a potentially fatal situation that brings the hero from her rock bottom, however, not without achieving new levels of realization and wisdom.

There are some key traits that every Hero has, and you may recognize yourself in some of those areas. Let's learn a little bit about the Hero:

Motto: Where there's a will, there's a way

Core desire: To come to know one's worth through courageous acts

Goal: Expert mastery in a way that improves the world

Greatest fear: Weakness, vulnerability, being a "chicken"

Strategy: To be as strong and competent as possible

Weakness: Arrogance, always needing another battle to fight

Talent: Competence and courage

The Hero is also known as: The warrior, crusader, rescuer, superhero, soldier, dragon slayer, winner and team player

According to Joseph Campbell, the Hero is born and raised in a rural setting away from cities. The origin of the Hero is mysterious. Sometimes the Hero loses her parents at a young age and is raised by animals or a wise guardian. The Hero returns to the land of his/her birth in disguise or as an unknown. The Hero is special, one of a kind. Your struggle as a Hero is for something valuable and important.

Characteristics of the Hero's Journey

You, the hero, are going about your life, minding your own business and outside the realm of your regular existence you are naïve to the fact that you are inexperienced. And yet you must face your deepest fears.

When you answer the Call to Adventure, you will leave the familiar world as you know it to this point, to enter an unfamiliar and challenging world. Look at the closest people in your life. Look beyond their guise of "normalcy," because the experience you are being brought to will bring out other aspects of everyone connected to you.

Everyone grows and benefits from your journey. There is a person who you might otherwise categorize as "strange." They are hard on you, put you through the ringer, will not allow you to wallow in a pity party because they know that greatness lies within you; they see it especially in the moments when you cannot. They hold the vision of your expanded self while you fumble and tumble around in the darkness, which is preparing you for what lies ahead.

You must go on a journey, learn lessons, transform in some way, return home and support the community you live in to rise higher than they had been.

Preparing for the Journey

I recommend that you spend time in quiet stillness several times a week so that you can identify the support that was sent to prepare you, even before the Call To Adventure comes to you. You are being helped by divine forces. You have guides.

Understand that your Hero's Journey is in fact a rite of passage or initiation, which is an event that marks the transformation from naïve and immature to a more mature understanding of the world.

Watch for a ritual or ceremony to take place either before or after your initiation. You will notice that a loyal band of companions surrounds you, supports you, protects you and provides you with much needed comic relief while you are in the trenches of personal transformation.

You will have to endure tests of strength (physical, emotional, spiritual and/or mental) and be able to demonstrate your new skill level despite suffering a potentially untreatable physical wound and at times, an emotional or spiritual wound from which you may never completely recover.

This journey of healing and transformation will be characterized by courage, strength and honor. You may even have to endure challenges that require you risk your life for the good of others in your tribe.

Are you ready? Let's begin!

And Create a New Life

1 The Ordinary World

Gift: Patience

Sacred Warrior Medicine: *"In my deepest, darkest moments, what really got me through was a prayer. Sometimes my prayer was 'Help me.' Sometimes a prayer was 'Thank you.' What I've discovered is that intimate connection and communication with my creator will always get me through, because I know my support, my help, is just a prayer away." ~Iyanla Vanzant*

My Call to Adventure

In 2011, my life was moving at the speed of light. I was coming off of the four most intense years of my life. In 2005, I started a rigorous two-year personal development program, which was followed by two years of ministerial training at the Inner Visions Institute for Spiritual Development in Silver Spring, Maryland under the tutelage of Rev. Dr. Iyanla Vanzant and her illustrious faculty.

During this training period, I took a deep look at myself and began to differentiate between who the world told me I was and who I had actually become on the inside. I did the arduous work of bringing those two distinct realities into alignment by literally re-creating my life. Little did I know that this soul-seeking, gut-wrenching work would dig up the bones of my past, open the doors and release the ghosts I had been living with. Doing this work also lightened the load that my heart was carrying--baggage that had never been mine.

At the end of this initiatory phase, came the ordination ceremony where my name was changed from Alicia Hill to Subira Folami. This is a Yoruba (Nigerian) name that means, "Patience. Respect and Honor me."

I thought it interesting that this new name was actually a directive. It was literally giving me instruction as to how I must relate to myself and my life moving forward. I also felt that this name raised the bar on how I must teach others to relate to me. This powerful name would become a lifeline for me.

From 2009 to 2011, I went about building a spiritual life coaching business, and quite frankly sleeping. My mind, my nervous system and my physical body had been completely rearranged, and I was exhausted to the bone. I regularly traveled between Maryland and Toronto, Canada.

I was finding my new rhythm as a newly ordained Minister of Spiritual Consciousness. I was also trying to figure out how I was going to offer my services to the world inclusive of this new aspect of myself, and on top of all of this, I was giving serious consideration to relocating to Canada.

December 11, 2011
8:34 a.m.

I crawled out of bed, shivering and ran to the shower. In the middle of December in Toronto, it was beyond freezing. As I turned on the water, I immediately began to thaw and bask in the heat, wishing I was in the tropics, but I wasn't.

I squeezed the sweet-smelling, liquid, shea butter, vanilla soap into the palm of my left hand and began to quickly rub my cold body. "Wash quickly, Alicia and you'll get warm faster!" I told myself.

As I passed over my right arm, shoulder and armpit, my hand landed on my right breast. *There was a lump.* Immediately, I heard a voice inside me say without hesitation: "You have cancer."

My breath stopped. I opened the shower curtain, dried off, walked into the living room and sat on the red and black couch that was on the far side of the room. I sat down next to my then-partner and placed her hand on my breast and began to cry.

No words needed to pass between us; she felt the lump too. She looked at me and said, "I am going to go through this with you." I promised that as soon as I returned home to Maryland, I would immediately go the doctor. The cold I had felt as I jumped from under the covers was going to be a constant companion for years to come.

My friends in the United States were already doing research on support services that could help me if it turned out I needed them. My friend Nina discovered that the state of Maryland had a Breast and Cervical Cancer Program. When I went into the doctor's office, I wasn't sure I would fit the list of stipulations to apply, however, the nurse (whose sister had died from breast cancer years earlier) suggested that I at least apply.

She reasoned that if it turned out I didn't have cancer, it wouldn't hurt me to at least have an application on file. I felt as though my head was being repeatedly thrust into a brick wall. Even though I could choose not to sit and fill out the paperwork, I knew that was not a wise choice. For the next two years, although I was always given options, I felt as though I had no choices.

I pulled out the chair and sat down at a small, round wooden table. I looked at the paperwork and each time I pressed the pen to paper and the ink flowed, so did my tears. I couldn't believe the questions I was answering were directed to me. I couldn't believe this stack of paper had words written on them that pertained to my body. The words that seemed to pulsate on the paper read: breast cancer. I remember a blue box of tissues. It was empty when I completed the application and my eyes were swollen.

The next morning, I woke up feeling a little bit more tired than normal. It was as if I were walking through a wall of mud. My heart was heavy. When the phone rang at 10:37 a.m., I almost jumped out of my skin. On the other end of the phone, my oncologist Dr. Ranieri was doing his best to speak calmly.

Dr. Ranieri: "Are you alone, Ms. Hill?"
Me: "Yes. I live alone."
Dr. Ranieri: "I see. Can you come into the office?"
Me: "Dr. Ranieri, do I have cancer? If I have cancer, I need you to say the words to me."

Dr. Ranieri: "Alright, have a seat. Ms. Hill, you have cancer."

The entire world went dead silent, and I could neither breathe nor move. From this moment and for the next three years, I felt frozen and like time stopped moving forward for me.

It was as if life had thrown a hand grenade to me and just as I caught it, it exploded. My entire world was floating in millions of tiny pieces all around me and I could not catch any of it. None of that life could ever come back together.

Unbeknownst to me, in those few moments, I had been catapulted from my Ordinary World into the next phase of the Hero's Journey. Life had just offered me the Call To Adventure, and I unwittingly accepted.

Although I was physically present, I could not feel. I went completely numb. It was as if my brain went into overload and shut down.

Looking back, I recognize that I had been plunged into the depths of peace. Everything was surreal, moving in slow motion. I heard sounds as if I were under water and my reactions were delayed. This new level of peace, which I initially understood as shock, preserved my nervous system by slowing me down.

Lesson of the White Belt: Servitude Before Mastery

If you want to overcome a situation, you have to be willing to give yourself over to it with a willingness to be awkward and unskilled.

In the Ordinary World, you are like most people, following the status quo. You are feeling settled as every day unfolds pretty much like the previous day. You may not feel excited about life. However, you are muddling along. You are not moving forward (mainly because you are unaware that there is a different experience of life you could be having if you choose it). Same thing, different day. You perceive monotony as safety.

What you don't know is that this world is your training ground for the initiations that are to come, as well as a place of rest every time you return home safely from the many initiations you will experience through your lifetime.

The Ordinary World may look something like this in your overall experience: You wake up in the morning, kiss your partner then stumble into the shower. Mentally, you run through the meetings you have ahead of you for the day, the emails you need to respond to and the calls you have to return.

You get dressed and make your way to the kitchen for a strong cup of liquid energy that you cannot start or make it through your workday without. You drive 30 to 60 minutes in bumper-to-bumper traffic, already wondering how in the world you will endure the 9 hours that are barreling down the pipe at you.

In those rare moments of quiet stillness when you are alone and being honest with yourself, you can acknowledge that an energy of quiet desperation has seized your life by the throat with a gentleness you have become so accustomed to yet, you are barely able to breathe.

Then you become fortunate enough to have the winds of transformation blow in your direction. You receive a phone call, an email or you are asked to sit down with someone you deeply care for to have a conversation.

What you don't know as you pick up the phone, open the correspondence or sit for the conversation, is that the winds of transformation have already come through your neighborhood and demolished the house

you were just standing in. Your life as you have
known it up to this point, is forever gone.

The first gift of initiation is commonly referred to as
shock. I want to offer you a new way of understanding
this phenomenon. I came to understand it as the gift of
peace in the eye of the storm, peace beyond my
previous understanding.

Once you dive into this emotional, spiritual and
mental depth and you learn to breathe under the
immense pressure that you find in the life-
transforming experiences of the Hero's Journey, the
gift of peace in the eye of the storm is yours forever.

Call forward this peace. You are free to take the deep
dive at any time and in any situation without fear
because you will know that you have learned to use
the tool of deep peace and very little will have the
ability to upset you.

When you say to the Universe that you desire to *be
more*, to expand the territory of both your inner and
outer landscapes, you need to know that you are going
to have to sit alone in the presence of your own
greatness. You will have to do this for some time so
that, that person can be born *in, as and through you.*

It doesn't matter if you desire to improve your relationship with your spouse, learn to offer and deliver more quality product or service, get a better job or complete that degree that you stopped working toward 20 years ago.

Whatever the vision you are carrying in your imagination, you need to understand that to do any of these things, you must become more. The only way to do that is by way of an initiation into the Hero's Journey. On this road, you will find that every resource, every person, and every bit of information you'll need, will be waiting for you as you walk down *your* path.

Every time you accept the invitation to initiation, expect chaos and confusion, expect to be thrust into the void. Know that is it inside the void, inside the womb, you are being incubated and every good thing that you require will be brought to you. Life is on your side and is conspiring that you conquer the seeming adversaries that you will encounter.

Many days during my 6.5 months of chemotherapy, I could clearly see that my years of daily spiritual practice deepened my patience for the long road ahead of me and taught me to respect the process I was in.

The Hero's Journey will thrust you into an odyssey so that you can deepen compassion for yourself and humanity, so that you can restore harmony to your corner of the world, so that you can keep expanding.

2 The Call to Adventure

Gift: Awareness and Strength

Sacred Warrior Medicine: *"That which does not kill us makes us stronger."~Friedrich Nietzsche*

My dear friend Cara-Michele immediately told me that she would go with me to the initial appointments. She was very wise and always reminded me in the beginning of my journey that we were doing nothing more that gathering information.

Every day for the first few weeks, I literally had three and sometimes four appointments with different doctors and lab technicians. They needed to know the type and size of cancer I was hosting in my breast and if it had moved into any of my organs or my lymphatic system.

I recall the mammogram. I moved as much of my B-cup sized breasts into the machine right up to my chest wall and held completely still while each breast was smashed flat. Even though it had already been established that my right breast had a tumor that extended the entire expanse of my relatively small breast, I still had to do the mammogram.

I cried as the machine clamped down on my very tender breasts. Little did I know, over the course of the next two years, I was going to learn to endure 24 hours of chronic, unbelievable, physical and emotional pain by consciously connecting with my breathing all day, every day.

When the mammogram was over, I wiped my eyes, took a few slow, deep breaths and went out to the waiting room. I felt as emotionally raw and tender as my right breast did after it was released from the compression that allowed the doctors to measure the tumor.

The nurses asked me to continue wearing the Pepto Bismol ®-colored smock that had only two buttons and opened in front. Cara-Michele and I waited for about 30 minutes. Finally, two nurses came out of the treatment room and the horrified looks on their faces said what their mouths did not. I am sure I looked dumbfounded.

They directed me back into the treatment room to get dressed and told me that I would need to go to the next step, which was a core biopsy. Whatever in the world those two words meant when placed together, I knew, could not be good.

I returned to the waiting room, feeling as though I had just been jumped into a gang. I told Cara-Michele the news; she must have seen the looks on the nurses' faces and on mine. She drew a deep breath, and like a soldier replied, "Okay, we need to get more information. It is too soon to respond."

She is so wise. Those words were planted in my heart and mind that day, and they took root. I heard her voice with each escalation of treatment, and for that, I am so very grateful. Within days, the core biopsy was done on my right breast. Tumor markers were inserted into the breast, giving the doctors landmarks around the tumor.

Finally came the day where I received the news of the stage of cancer I was hosting: Stage 1. I thought, "Okay, this could have been much worse. They'll do a lumpectomy, and I'll be back to my life."

Cara-Michele is an acupuncturist who owns and operates a clinic in Baltimore called, Strength & Vitality Wellness Center. She suggested I get a thermal scan in her clinic, which I was happy to do mainly because it had just the peaceful atmosphere my nervous system needed.

The thermal scan was the only gentle and non-invasive procedure I would experience for the next two years. The technician looked at the scan and almost too quickly told me that she could not give me the results of the scan.

They had to be sent off to the Mayo Clinic in Minnesota and the doctors there would contact me with my results. She followed that up with, "I wish you the best of luck, Ms. Hill." The look of sadness in her eyes, the strain in her voice and the heat markings that engulfed my entire right breast on the screen told me everything she legally could not verbally say to me: I had cancer and this looked bad.

During each subsequent procedure, every needle used to extract tissue or to push some other chemical into my body to assist the medical staff in seeing, measuring and understanding the lethal level of the tumor, was larger than the one before.

This was quickly becoming a problem. I was "that kid" who screamed bloody murder and who needed to be held down whenever it was time to get a shot. "That kid" was about to overcome this deep-seated fear that I had been living with for 41 years.

I distinctly recall waking up one morning, and I could

not speak. My mind was numb. Working was not an option. And as a spiritual life coach, if I was not taking on coaching clients, I was no longer bringing in an income. What could I do?

I could barely get my mouth open. I was not able to put sentences together. My body was somehow moving from place to place, and I do not remember telling it to stand or sit or walk or stop. This was when I experienced a visceral understanding of the need to create sustainable residual income streams.

Within a very short timeframe, my friends Nina and Tanya joined forces to start a GoFundMe campaign to make sure that at least some of my monthly financial obligations stayed current. However, the weight of the financial pressure soon began breaking through the protective barrier of the financial donations. Within a few months, I could no longer pay my mortgage, and I found myself asking Nina to negotiate on my behalf with my mortgage company, which was contacting me every day.

My home went into foreclosure and stayed there for two straight years. I would end up standing in line at the social services office applying for food stamps and assistance to keep my utilities paid. All the while, on a daily basis, I was going from one oncology appointment to another. The pressure blew my mind into what felt like millions of tiny little pieces.

Lesson of White Belt: Servitude Before Mastery

If you want to overcome a situation, you have to be willing to give yourself over to it with a willingness to be awkward and unskilled.

When you find yourself right in the middle of a situation that you cannot believe is real, however, every time you close your eyes and reopen them, the unbelievable situation is staring back at you … rest assured you have answered the Call to Adventure. And the answer you gave was, "Yes, I accept. I will go."

While you may not consciously remember agreeing to go on this adventure, I want you to remember that there are two parts of you at work all the time with regard to your personal development. There is the part that wants nothing more than to grow and to leave behind the constriction of the scared version of yourself.

This part of you is the bold, daring Hero. She knows that if she could just get you to experience courage, together you and she would become the grand vision you spend all day dreaming and scheming about. However, because of fear, you never actually take the steps that are required.

The lessons at this stage center around teaching you, Sacred Warrior, how to heighten your awareness, sharpen your intuition and build your strength for the arduous journey ahead. The Call to Adventure is about confronting your largest fears.

You are not expected to slay your dragons, yet. However, you are going to have to develop the strength to look them square in the face and identify them. Usually, these fears center around issues like fear of the unknown, death, isolation and loss of safety. To continue growing, evolving and moving forward, you will have to face what you fear.

As your Guide and Mentor, I want you to know, that from this point on, the work you must do happens first on the inside. *The place you must go and the monsters that will arise all have their beginning and ending inside your mind.* And it is here that you must serve the fear by facing it so that you can overcome it.

Your body may very well need to endure pain, but I need you to remember, in those moments that your breath and the power that resides in your heart and mind will get you to the other side of all of the fear.

Sacred Warrior, you will know you have received the Call To Adventure when you no longer recognize yourself and the day-to-day unfolding of your life. It's that moment when everything around you falls apart and try as hard as you might, you cannot keep it from unraveling. If you find yourself pinching yourself to see if, perhaps, you are in the deepest darkest part of an extremely bad dream or if you find yourself asking, "Is this *my* life? How did I get here?", that is when you will know that you accepted the Call to Adventure.

Your Relationships *Will* Change

In the beginning, the people from your Ordinary World will surround you. However, it is important for you to know and eventually accept that even that will transform. Even if some of these people remain in your life as you move forward through your Hero's Journey, everyone involved, even if they are simply watching you go through it, will be transformed.

Relationships that you thought would be your bedrock may eventually crumble under the weighty demands of transformation. On the other hand, relationships you never would have imagined being solid will end up being your safe space, the soft place you can rest.

These surprising relationships will reveal themselves to be your protection during your most vulnerable moments.

In the Call To Adventure, you will at first become disoriented and you will feel probably the most vulnerable you've felt since being a baby. This is the exact training ground that is required for Life and Love to cultivate awareness and strength in you.

How else to feel and understand the subtle messages swirling around you in nature all the time and how else to become strong except to have intense daily practice with the teachers, Awareness and Strength? Your acceptance of the Call To Adventure is surely a way.

As you wake up and find yourself in a world that is suddenly unknown to you, take courage and know that you are being thrust into confusion, chaos and darkness for a specific purpose. You replied, "yes!" to a call for which you have been both prepared and *preserved*.

Indeed, Life and Love have actually been serving you. Your former level of awareness was not mature enough to allow you to see your circumstances from this meta-physical (above the physical) perspective.

You are a Warrior, and warriors only go into battle for noble causes.

You have stepped onto the battleground of transformation for the noble cause of finally slowing down. Or to literally sit still for a period of time and allow yourself to become aware of the energy patterns in your life. You will notice those that serve you and those that no longer serve you so that you can live fully and unapologetically in alignment for your purpose. *You are precious*. The Call To Adventure is the point in the transformation process that allows you to know that this is indeed the truth.

And Create a New Life

3 Refusal of the Call

Gift: Discernment

Sacred Warrior Medicine: *"We should not fret for what is past, nor should we be anxious about the future; (people) of discernment deal only with the present moment."~Chanakya*

January 16, 2012
10 a.m.

I sat in the naturopath's, office for the third time. This was the day after being told that I had been mis-staged and that I actually had stage 3 breast cancer. I had the file that the oncologist gave me explaining everything.

As I sat waiting for the naturopath to see me, I allowed only small streams of breath to escape my body. I was thinking, "I don't know how many breaths I have left to my name." The day before, the floor caved in beneath my feet, and I was officially tumbling downward into a black hole of confusion, disorder and disbelief.
Ever since I sat in the office with the oncologist who told me that I had been given the wrong staging, no

one's words made sense. My world was rocked. I asked my friend, Ari to go with me to the appointment for three very distinct reasons:

1. She overcame stage 1 breast cancer, so I knew that she could help me navigate all of this.
2. She was about 30 years older than me and in my mind, she felt like a mom and I really wanted my mom at this point.
3. She had an extremely strong Buddhist practice and was energetically as steady as a rock. I needed people around me who felt solid and grounded.

Now the naturopathic doctor pulled out a large book, you know, the big colorful ones that are very shiny with thick pages, big print and even bigger and very colorful pictures to help her, help me.

The book was supposed to help me hear that I was carrying stage 3 CANcer in my right breast, and the reason it was stage 3 is because they found cancer in my lymph nodes … blah, blah, blah.

My head was spinning as she pointed to the pictures of the breast and the ducts. I looked over at Ari who was sitting in a chair to my right with her hand over her mouth and tears so thick they threatened to fall at any moment. She looked horrified. I felt like I was going to vomit all over the doctor.

This can't be right, this can't be right, this cannot be right!

Inside I was screaming and crying, but no tears would fall, and I refused to give up or *give in* to this diagnosis. Surely there had to be a natural treatment plan that Dr. Martin could find for me. I'd heard how people ate fruits and drank interesting teas made with exotic herbs and their CANcer was cured. My mind told me that if it was possible for those people, it had to be possible for me too.

Unfortunately, that was not the case. Instead, I sat as Dr. Martin talked to me in very low tones using very compassionate word choices. My mind refused to bend to the direction of the words that were coming out of her mouth.

I said, "Can't we change my diet? I will eat only raw foods. Anything but chemo."

She then explained it to me with these exact words that I will never forget:

> "Alicia, I would be doing you a disservice. We would have had to make those changes 10

years ago. It is too late. Doing anything else at this point would be like me standing outside of a burning building and praying when we need to be hosing it down with water. What we can do is protect your gut as you go through this process and then help to rebuild your body after the treatments."

I was a building on fire that required nothing less than emergency medical attention. However, I felt as cold as the frozen tundra.

For several more months, my mind, heart and mouth would bargain with all of the physicians as I looked for any conceivable way out of walking down this unbelievably ghastly path that was quickly taking shape and form right in front of me.

In my mind, I was powerful enough to withstand the treatments I would be given, and so on my first trip to the chemotherapy infusion clinic, I brought a lawyer-style briefcase that contained my laptop, books and phone.

I was going to be the one who could work through six months of weekly chemotherapy treatments. Needless to say, by my third week of treatment, I was bundled up like a baby in the infusion chair for 6 and sometimes 8 hours as poison coursed through my veins, and some very strong pills put me right to sleep. On top of that, I would have seven blood transfusions in six months.

White Belt Lesson: Servitude Before Mastery

If you want to overcome a situation, you have to be willing to give yourself over to it with a willingness to be awkward and unskilled.

Sacred Warrior, you have reached a point wherein although you feel confused about what is happening, you also have come to grips with the fact that you are at the threshold of some sort of change. What you are now clear about is that you must face this change, you have to make a choice whether to keep moving forward or to remain in your current situation.

The challenge is that you feel like you do not have a choice or that you are being asked to choose between bad and worse. Either way, you have to decide. However, it is at this point in the Hero's Journey that you will Refuse the Call and it's perfectly alright. You are supposed to, that is one of the milestones on the journey.

Your Mind's Role

Understand, my fellow traveler, even you saying to yourself, "I can't do this" is part of the unfolding of your transformative process. Every Hero is faced with a challenge that is designed to overwhelm your mind. This must happen. The internal milestones that you are facing here are fear, resistance and change.
Your mind is the communication and control system between you and your environment. It's constantly busy solving problems it perceives (correctly or incorrectly) that make you feel as though your safety and survival are at risk. Since you were taught that the purpose of the mind is to solve problems, you erroneously believe that the higher your intellect, the better the use of your mind and this is not completely accurate.

The challenge with this is that oftentimes, your mind connects pictures to meanings and creates pairings that do not serve your highest and best good. The stories and interpretations that your mind arrives at many times will give you "cause for pause" and that pause can last so long that you end up stagnant in your life.

The uncertainty and perceived danger ahead is the next stop on your journey.

What you need to know is that when you face a situation that you cannot break or bend, when the situation is literally unfolding *in you, through you*, and *as you*, there is no escaping. It has come to you because it is your path, because for your life's purpose to be realized, you have to go through this initiation.

When Life first sends out the Call To Adventure with your name on it, you will most likely experience cognitive dissonance (the mental distress caused by holding contradictory beliefs, ideas, or values at the same time). The fact is that the version of the life you've been comfortably or uncomfortably living changed on a dime and you simply were not ready. The truth is, there is no way to prepare for the initiation of transformation and expansion that you are about to undergo.

So go ahead, Beloved, refuse the call. The call already knows that you must refuse it so that you can one day surrender to the path and your life's purpose. Only then will your mind loosen the tight grip it has on your former life and outdated understanding.

If someone could have given you advance warning that transformation was coming and had let you in on the magnitude of it, your heart could not have taken this information in and your mind would not have understood what was being said. Life already knows that and spares you those moments of disbelief knowing that it will meet you in the state of disbelief shortly anyway.

You instinctively know that this place is dangerous and you cannot believe that the only way out of this situation, is directly through it. However, that is the case. Expect fear, resistance and transformation to show up front and center. They are the Worthy Opponents that have to somehow convince you to get up and face them. These energies are charged with the task of training you how to release the fight from your mind and to surrender it to your spirit, the life force energy that has sustained you up to this point.

Fear has got to be frightening enough to challenge you, yet not so frightening that you stop moving forward. Resistance has got to show up in your life and apply enough pressure so that you press back without applying so much pressure that the challenge feels immovable. And finally, transformation must shapeshift with a degree of grace that almost makes the change feel unnoticeable while you are traveling through it. However, transformation also needs to have been so remarkable that when you *do* complete your Hero's Journey, you have a challenging time recognizing even yourself.

No wonder when you find yourself in this situation, you do not want to say yes to the invitation that life is offering you! From the outside, the offer looks like something even the most naïve person would decline. Yet there is a voice inside of you that accepts the invitation and moves forward.

It is as if your mind shuts down and your gut instincts begin to take over. This is a good thing because even though you don't know it quite yet, one of the lessons that you will learn on your Hero's Journey will be to hone your intuition.

By refusing the call to move forward, life is given the opportunity to train you in the masterful skill of intuitive guidance, and I assure you that you can always trust your intuition.

And Create a New Life

4 Meeting With The Mentor

Gift: Love

Sacred Warrior Medicine: *"You can search throughout the entire universe for someone who is more deserving of your love and affection than you are yourself, and that person is not to be found anywhere. You yourself, as much as anybody in the entire universe deserve your love and affection."*
~Buddha

September 2011

About six years before, I started to have this knowing feeling in my gut that I would be serving people virtually. Now you've got to understand that I literally did not know how to even send a text in 2005! I scoffed at the vision, because although I intuitively understood the value of the Internet, I had no frame of reference for technology and quite frankly, the thought of learning technology frightened me.

In college, I studied the Humanities. I'm a people person. I equated technology with math, which I only took to matriculate. However, I'm a *Star Wars*, *Star Trek* and anything Sci-Fi fan. So, a shift happened inside me where I began to see all of the amazing places technology could take me and all of the connections that could be made.

I began to see that I could design my life based on the vision that started to become more and more clear as I became more open and accepting of technology. The moment I opened myself up was the moment my mentors started appearing. They came before I even knew I was hosting cancer and began teaching me skills that would become invaluable one year later, two years later, three years later. So let me introduce you to just a few of my mentors:

Diane Hochman

Diane Hochman teaches people who work from home, how to generate an income based on the Internet. In September 2011, Diane opened up a three-month training session where she taught an online marketing course. She would teach me things I did not know I was going to need in 2012 and 2013.

I went into this thinking that I just wanted to learn how to make money online. Little did I know that Diane was going to give the class an assignment that would help to shift the trajectory of my life and my life path: cut 90 videos in 90 days and post them to your YouTube channel. I didn't know that this assignment would support me through two years of treatment.

Once treatment started, friends started calling me every day, because they were afraid. They were dealing with a whole host of emotions, and most of them could not get here to be with me in person, so they were calling me.

I was dealing with *my own anxiety, pain and fear,* so I decided to cut a video updating people about my progress as often as I could. I would share how I was feeling about what I was going through and about what my needs were.

The videos I posted on my YouTube channel led to an international outpouring of love and support for me. Because my channel existed, it connected me to other women on the breast cancer treatment journey and served as another resource of insight, inspiration, encouragement and hope for these women.

Making videos gave me an outlet for my emotions because it became my journal. Another amazing thing that was happening, unbeknownst to me, was that I was learning to organically guide traffic to where I wanted them to go on the Internet. And when I needed financial assistance, it came; when I needed my yard mowed, it came; when I needed groceries, they came; when I needed help with utilities, it came; when I needed help getting to the doctor, someone came and on and on and on.

At times I was just barely able to keep my head above water, but Diane gave me this very practical skill. She also assigned me a book that was full of mindset training called *Ten Feet Tall and Bulletproof* by Joe Schroder. I would read the title over and over and over, and tell myself again and again, "I'm 10 feet tall and bulletproof." For two years, the gift of this book seared into my brain some of the most important principles that I needed to know.

So I am forever grateful to Diane, my mentor, for planting the seeds.

Tanya

Tanya is an ICU nurse and an elite copywriter. During her night shift, literally in the Midnight Hour, when she wasn't with a client or when she wasn't with a patient, she was texting me. Night time was the hardest for me. I lived alone, and there were times where I literally didn't know if I was going to live to see the sunrise. The pain was just that bad.

I didn't know what awaited me in certain procedures. I had this deep fear of intubation and being in the hospital because I had never been sick before--not to this degree. So I was able to talk to Tanya and tell her my deepest, darkest fears in the deepest, darkest parts of the night via text. She was a lifeline for me.

It got to the point that when funds needed to be raised to help me keep my home, Tanya pulled out her magic wand as I like to call it. There is power in the pen for sure and she wrote the most amazing letter that went with my Gofund Me account. Money poured in. Meanwhile, my responsibility was to, as much as possible, continue to cut a video as often as I could. With those two things, at least I was able to keep my head above water.

Alethea

I came in contact with Alethea after she completed her breast cancer treatments and as I was beginning mine. It was with Alethea that I had the conversation that only another breast cancer survivor is going to understand. She understood the nuances of the fear, the anxiety, the heartbreak--she understood it all. She prayed with me and spoke to me, and we came to have this deep friendship without ever seeing each other in person the entire two years of my treatment process.

We spoke on the phone every day and usually we spoke on the phone several times a day. She too became a lifeline. She gave me new ways to see the process that I was in. She gave me the compassionate ear of someone who had been there. She gave me foresight, which prepared me, so I didn't have to go into the process in complete darkness. Although I did have to go in alone, there was a sliver of light and that sliver of light was Alethea.

Lori

The hospital where I was treated has a program where women who are entering breast cancer treatment receive a mentor, someone they can call at anytime who's going to understand. I remember talking with Lori many times, usually while she was in the middle of her workday.

I remember calling her and telling her how afraid I was, she gave me such comfort. I remember one day I was having my chemotherapy treatment and in walks this short blonde woman with this huge smile on her face. She walked over and she gave me a big hug. Just an hour before, she was on the operating table having the port removed from her chest. Her breast cancer treatment Journey was complete, but she knew that mine was just beginning. She took the time to come by and give me some encouragement. I'm grateful, Lori. Thank you.

The Inner Visions Institute for Spiritual Development

I did the most in-depth spiritual development training between the years 2005 and 2009 at the Inner Visions Institute for Spiritual Development. I like to call it a four-year spiritual boot camp. During my time there, I went through a two-year personal development program that challenged everything about myself that I thought was small, inadequate, unworthy and less than. The program challenged the places where I lied to myself and accepted less from myself than who I was and what I was capable of.

Upon graduation from that two-year personal development program, I entered the ministry program for another two years of in-depth study about God, the universe, the laws of the universe, service and so many more things.

This is where I began to get clear on how all of my interests all work together, not only for my good but also for the good of the people that I am on the planet to serve. After this program, I had clarity about my ministry and the fact that my work is about offering hope and healing and an intimate understanding of the power of God.

Little did I know that two years after my ordination, I would be thrust into one of the deepest physical, emotional, mental, spiritual and relational healing periods of my life. Rev. Iyanla Vanzant, along with her faculty and staff, spent four years preparing me for this journey.

Reverend Dorothy

At the age of 41, I had to sit down and decide how I wanted things to be handled should I die on the operating table or at any other point in the process. I had to think of how I want my affairs handled if I were to end up in a vegetative state or if I were to go into a coma.

Thinking on these end-of-life matters was a paralyzing process, and day after day, week after week, Rev. Dorothy, a woman of the cloth and an attorney, would come to my home. I could only think about these things in small spurts then I would emotionally break down. So we would sometimes only answer one question on the packet that the hospital gave me to fill out prior to surgery.

In the most compassionate, patient and loving way, Dorothy extended herself, mentored me through this process and prepared me to talk about and face my death head on. She walked me through that very, very difficult process and for that I am so humbled and forever grateful.

Professor Jamal

As a martial artist, exercise has always been very important to me, so while I was thinking about moving to Toronto, I began looking for a way to study both yoga and martial arts. I stumbled upon a guy named Jamal who practiced Budokon, which looked like the perfect combination of both. I gave him a call, and he told me that although his Facebook page at the time showed him in Canada, he no longer lived there. I asked him where, he said, "I'm in the United States. I'm in Maryland and I live in this little town you probably never heard of." And I said, "Well that's weird cuz I live in Maryland."

So at the time of course I was really sad, because I was just trying to get all of my ducks in a row so that I'd have somewhere to train when I moved to Canada.

Months later, I was in treatment in Maryland and starting to mentally crawl the walls because I couldn't exercise, I discovered that Professor Jamal's yoga studio was not that far from after all! When I walked in, I'm sure I looked like the walking dead. I had no hair and my skin was gray. I had lost at least 20 pounds if not more.

I was weak and tired, but I knew I needed this to help me keep my mind focused and give my body the message that it was still alive and strong and it was going to be okay. I told Professor Jamal that I needed him to train me.

He looked at me and said, "Let's start training." He was very, very gentle and for the most part, we focused on lower body exercises. For months in the gym, it was Professor Jamal and me in a one-on-one old-school, martial arts mentorship. He became my Mr. Miyagi. He became a definite Lifeline for my body and my mind. He gave me a place to go to feel strong, and he learned over time when to push me and when to be gentle. He helped me figure out a way to sit in this most uncomfortable body that was being broken down and then taught me how to build it back up. For that I am grateful.

Rev. Dr. Kathy "Chioma" Gainor

I was in my kitchen doing dishes during my cancer treatments when I had a stroke. Even though I was surrounded by friends at the time, Chioma jumped in her car and drove three hours from her home state to be by my side.

In my nuclear family, I am the first-born child, which makes me a big sister. During this healing journey, I was blessed with Chioma as my "big sister." Chioma has been my faithful friend and as steady as a rock.

She has made sure that I have always had what I needed, including a shoulder to cry on before, during and after doctors' visits. My dear sister-friend has always allowed me to go deep within without feeling like I was shrinking during this process. For Chioma, I'm truly grateful.

Love

Love was my mentor from 2006 to 2012. Love taught me how to give patience, honor, respect, loyalty and commitment to another person. It taught me to live my vision. Love taught me to embrace it, to expand, to try new things to love bigger, wider and deeper than I ever knew was possible. And then love released me to give all of that love and the fruits of all of those lessons to myself as I continued on the path from 2012 to the present, and for that lesson, I am grateful.

Breast Cancer

Your mentors will not always show up as a person. Many times it will be the journey itself or the situation that will be your biggest mentor and teach you your toughest lessons so that you become the person you were meant to be on this planet.

Breast cancer has been my biggest and most challenging mentor. Breast cancer has scarred my chest. It has changed my cellular makeup. It has wiped my slate completely clean and clear.

The process to heal from cancer required my initiation with poison and fire and water and earth and air. Breast cancer taught me and continues to teach me about the world, other people, love, forgiveness, patience, humility, service and compassion.

It taught me how to find my voice and use it. It taught me how to use my eyes in a way I had never used them before, to see the vision and the truth of who I am. It showed me the path for how I am to become what I see in the vision. It taught me sacredness. It taught me how to be gentle. It taught me how to be a warrior.

Lesson of Red Belt: Principles, Practice and Living

At this rank you begin to understand that by governing your life through principles, you become more stable in you thoughts and emotions. By developing a regular practice, you can see the possibility of relating to your life as a piece of art.

At this point, you are now firmly on your path. You may or may not have come to terms with the fact that you are no longer in your Ordinary World, that place where everybody knew your name and you felt safe and comfortable.

Life as you knew it has been reduced to tiny shreds of bits and pieces. You feel like you are looking at the world's largest jigsaw puzzle--24,000 pieces--if not more, are asking for your attention. Very quickly you realize that putting them together will be an exercise that would send the best minds running for the hills. However, you are a Sacred Warrior, so you move forward in a different energy.

As a Sacred Warrior, you know that it is best to become still and survey your environment. You know that you will be best served if you sit and listen to your internal messages and for clues that will guide you to your next steps. You will find yourself feeling restless and afraid and unsure of yourself.

You begin to question your abilities as well as your motives. Deep down, you are imagining that the person who left home not so long ago, is not up to facing the challenges at this point in your journey.

That's when your mentor shows up just in time to offer you training, insight into the dilemma you are facing, companionship, advice or an object of great significance when it looks like you are at the end of your rope.

He reminds you that eventually, we all have to learn life's lessons from someone or something and that you already have everything you need inside yourself. The only thing missing was that mentor who can support you, as you unlock your dormant potential.

Know that although your training at this point will be tough, your mentor is actually in your life to dispel any doubts, confusion and fears that you are wrestling with and to give you the strength and courage to go that much deeper into your vision quest.

It is the energy of the mentor archetype that will push you past your own fear sending you into the adventure. The mentor shows up after you've accepted the adventure, struck out and found yourself at your wit's end, because you were not yet equipped to handle the situations you have found yourself in.

Within the boundaries of this relationship, you will have to face the core relationship dynamics and bond that exist between parent and child, teacher and student, doctor and patient, God and man. It will be close to impossible to fully develop into the Hero if you do not confront, and on some levels, heal any psychological hurts that you may be holding against your mother and or your father.

To grow in confidence to the point that you are able to face your "dark night of the soul," you will have to grow up emotionally, psychologically and spiritually. And the mentor, although not your parent, will represent your parents and give you the opportunity to work out any core issues so that you can forgive your parents for things they did or did not do during your childhood.

The mentor, a sometimes harsh but always protective person, is tasked with giving you the supplies, the knowledge, the confidence through a usually rigorous period of training. They will then put you to the test to see if you are truly ready to put fear and doubt behind you before you head out into the unknown journey.

While you are looking at your life for the mentor, I caution you not to look only for people. Be mindful that *your mentor can be just about anything, including an experience*. Sometimes they will be obvious, sometimes subtle.

When you find your back against the wall, look for this wise person to appear, seemingly out of nowhere, or an auspicious circumstance that suddenly helps you escape.

It is time for you to look a little deeper into your life. Look with new eyes at the people who are surrounding you. They are preparing you and giving you the skills that you need to make it through the long and arduous parts of the journey.

And Create a New Life

5 Crossing the Threshold

Gift: Power

Sacred Warrior Medicine: *"When you start to develop your powers of empathy, transparency and imagination, the whole world opens up to you."~Sensei Subira*

January 26, 2012
8 a.m.
Day 1 of Chemotherapy

It was a very early morning, and I was not yet quite awake. It was freezing outside. The cold felt really good, but I was emotionally numb.

When I walked into the infusion clinic for my chemotherapy treatment, there were two other patients. Reverend Rosetta was with me to my right. She sat down and opened her Bible and *A Course in Miracles*. My nurse wheeled over a cart. I looked over and saw IV bags marked with a skull and crossbones.

The nurse reached down to the bottom drawer of her cart and pulled out an overall. She then covered her hair and stepped into the overall and put her arms through a jacket. Next, she put on safety goggles, a mask over her nose and mouth, gloves and booties over her shoes.

She told me to relax. After watching her suit up to protect herself against the poison she was about to push into my body, I didn't know how I was supposed to relax. She asked, "Are you ready?"

I knew once she pushed the needle into my chest, there was no turning back. She pulled the curtain around my chair so that I could have some privacy, and I said, "Yes I'm ready."

And then this previously very sweet woman pulled out a needle and aimed it at my chest. I had put on some numbing cream, but that didn't help. The port was not functioning properly. She got no blood return.

I had stepped across the Threshold. It was my first experience with a failed port. She kept trying to get blood return, but it wasn't happening. She tried everything at her disposal. She had other nurses come over to help her, but it still wasn't working.

All the while Reverend Rosetta sat by my side as I clamored and held onto a big green infusion chair for dear life. My nurse then announced that they would need to push the chemo drugs through my arm. I told her I could not do that.

First of all, I was deathly afraid of needles. The fact that one was going through my chest and I could feel it was already more than my mind was comfortable taking. I cried. I asked if we could get another port and start the chemo another day. She told me that we were on a very strict schedule and that we *had* to go forward today.

So I crossed over the Threshold during my first chemo treatment. Somehow I made it through that painful experience. I did get a new port put in the following week. And every week for six and a half months, I sat in that infusion chair.

Lesson of the Red Belt: Principles, Practice and Living

At this rank you begin to understand that by governing your life through principles, you become more stable in you thoughts and emotions. By developing a regular practice, you can see the possibility of relating to your life as a piece of art.

This is the moment of truth. This moment is asking you, the Hero-In-Training, a singular question: Are you committed to transformation? Although this question may be verbal, your verbal response will not be enough.

At this juncture on your journey, you *must* take action. You must step into the unknown. You must cross over the threshold completely. That is the only way to show that you are committed. Because once you take this step, there is absolutely no turning back. You cannot unring this bell. I am here to tell you that saying "yes" and taking the steps forward is not for the faint of heart.

Luckily, the journey already knows that the Hero-In-Training will be afraid. It is as if you are standing at the precipice of a dark tunnel or a huge cliff and there's nowhere else to go except to step off the cliff and into the darkness.

Of course, at every gate, there will be Gatekeepers tasked with testing you one final time before you move forward. They will test you to make sure that all of your mentors have given you all of the appropriate tools and supplies and that you have learned the lessons you need.

Sometimes these Gatekeepers appear to be adversaries, opponents or resistors to your forward movement, but that's not really their intention. Their intention is to make sure that before you cross this threshold, you are prepared because quite honestly the Hero's Journey will require that parts of you undergo a death.

Sometimes even your physical death might be in the balance, but for sure there will be parts of the way you think, process feelings, deal with your spirituality and the way you were in a relationship with yourself and others, that will have to be completely transformed. You will be a completely different person by the time this journey is complete, and so the threshold Gatekeepers ensure you are ready.

Make sure that you have support with you that can bolster you and ground you because no one can make this step for you. They can be at the threshold, they can wait outside the gate, but not even The Gatekeepers go through the gate. Only the Hero-in-Training, the Sacred Warrior, is allowed to pass through the gate and continue on the journey.

Here you will learn empathy and compassion. You will learn to be transparent with yourself, at the very least about the truth of what you feel, because this will give you the gift of deeper intuition.

By taking the physical steps to cross the threshold, you are sending a very strong symbolic message to your mind, heart, body and the people around you: that you have now entered a rite of passage and there is no turning back. By moving forward, you state your intentionality and commitment to yourself and the world.

This is a defining moment in your life. This is a moment of independence *and* responsibility. This is where you are demonstrating your willingness and ability to step fully up to the plate and to stand fully in your life, come what may.

Stepping into the world this way is a bold and daring act. You are going from being a child at home where everything is known to you and comfortable to stepping out as an adult into the unknown. Into what is going to surely be unpredictable and dangerous.

In this new world, you have to learn the new rules because they are completely different from the

Ordinary World that you have come from. Somehow, intuitively you know that the cost of failure is high.

Acknowledge that moment where you know you are crossing over to that point of no return. Acknowledge those who are supporting you. Acknowledge the strength that you have. You could not be a weak person and cross the threshold. You could not be a weak person and face adversaries that look like monsters and the unknown. You could not be weak and walk into the darkness not knowing what is going to meet you directly on the other side.

I want you to acknowledge yourself. I want you to give yourself credit. Watch the music video *Champion* for yourself on Youtube and congratulate yourself for having crossed the Threshold.

And Create a New Life

6 Tests, Allies & Enemies

Gift: Imagination

Sacred Warrior Medicine: *"I saw the angel in the marble and carved until I set him free."~Michelangelo*

January 13, 2012
7:25 p.m.

I wasn't expecting company when my doorbell rang. I was in the kitchen doing dishes while feeling very much dazed and confused. I opened the door to find a tall, slender woman standing there asking if she could come in and talk to me for a few minutes.

Even though I was in an emotional fog, I did recognize her from the Buddhist community I had been chanting with every morning and evening for the previous two years. She reminded me that her name was Crystal Cleer, (a name that would prove to be very apropos in the coming years). We sat together on the floor in front of my fireplace, and she commenced to make the boldest request from me that I have ever, to this day, had to consider.

Crystal told me the story of her mother, who died from breast cancer years earlier and how she had not been able to be present for her mother in the way she would have liked. She asked if I would give her permission to walk on this journey with me. She told me that in this way she felt that she could do for me what she was unable to do for her mother.

I had just met my sidekick.

Crystal made certain that she was at every doctor's appointment with me. She advocated for me with the doctors and on the days when I felt that I just could not go on, she came over and crawled on the couch with me (the vastness of my bed felt like an ocean that would swallow me whole and so I slept on my couch all of 2012 and 2013). She held me as I cried and agreed that this was a shitty experience, and she always reminded me that I was going to be okay.

She would leave after the medication had taken their full effect and I had cried myself to sleep, only to show up the next morning with a big ol' grin on her face saying, "Well, it's time to go to the hospital!"

I would painstakingly walk to the car and go in for yet another unbelievably horrific treatment. Knowing that in a few hours I would be sick as a dog again, my sidekick was there no matter what. She would laugh, cry, sing, be silly and when I needed it, Crystal was my soldier. She came with gifts of flowers picked from her garden, food that she'd prepared by hand, music, dance and bedazzled jewelry.

Lesson of the Red Belt: Principles, Practice and Living

At this rank you begin to understand that by governing your life through principles, you become more stable in you thoughts and emotions. By developing a regular practice, you can see the possibility of relating to your life as a piece of art.

Life is all about growth, and oftentimes the one component that helps us grow is struggle and conflict. Since you have stepped into the role of Hero-in-Training, just about everything that comes up in your life at this point will revolve around you moving toward your ultimate vision. You might say that you are on what the Native Americans call a vision quest.

You will find yourself tested, and many times thwarted until you have learned many lessons and overcome many obstacles. For this reason the next stop on your journey is known as "tests, allies and enemies." It is very similar to crossing the first threshold. At this stage of your initiation, there will be other tasks that you must complete, more thresholds to cross, more guardians who you have to learn to work with and, very often, you may have to defeat them. Always remember that these tests are happening to support you in growing and developing so that when the ultimate battle comes, you are fully trained and prepared.

In this new world, you will need a posse, a team or a community. During your training, you're going to discover who your allies are and who your worthy opponents are.

At this stage in the game, you are learning the skill of discernment. Learning to trust yourself is one of your tests, and as your ability to do that increases, it will be much easier for you to know who can be trusted in this new world.

Your allies could be those who end up traveling with you. However, while you pass each test, you will find yourself being of support to other people who are also on the journey. They may not travel with you the entire way, but somewhere down the road these people will show up in your life again, and they will be of service to you. And that is an amazing thing.

Knowing this allows you to travel lightly and not hold on to relationships for dear life. This understanding allows you to go with the flow in terms of your relationships, understanding that people come into your life usually for a season, always for a reason and rarely for a lifetime. The sooner that you can accept that Sacred Warrior, the easier navigating your life's journey will be.

At this juncture, pay special attention to that one person who is your "ride or die" ally. You can call this person your sidekick. The sidekick typically is the one person devoted to you, the Hero, and this is the person who you can count on to be with you throughout most of your vision quest. She often enters the journey when you feel most alone and are preparing to enter the darkest days of the journey.

This person will serve as your voice of reason when you begin to doubt or think too highly of yourself. This person will act as the voice of your conscience when you're about to make decisions, and this person is the one who acts as a clown. This will be the person who brings the gift of laughter, music, dance and generally a good time. She can lighten your load for you by offering a different way to see the tough terrain; she often points out the silver lining.

Whatever you do, *do not take your sidekick lightly*.
This is someone extremely special who has his or her
own deep-seated issues and unfinished business with
the Universe. It just so happens that your odyssey is
comprehensive enough that she can see herself finally
tackling her own unfinished business by playing a
supportive role for you.

As always, there will be tests and seeming enemies
that you must subdue and it is your ally, who becomes
the wind beneath your wings. Look for that person
who you come to consider irreplaceable, like a big
sister or little brother.

Your sidekick is there to serve you and make sure you
do not get stuck in the muck, the mire and the
heaviness of the situation that you absolutely must
make it through. Look at the people in your life who
have a mission that is so large, that the only way they
can accomplish theirs is to be supportive of another
person's, and she has chosen you.

The sidekick will sometimes play the role of your
mentor, especially if someone important in your life
cannot continue on this path with you.

Your sidekick will help you use your imagination. She

will call your inner child out to play, and this will give your mind relief. Your sidekick, although playing the fool for you Hero-in-Training, is extremely wise and has a heightened awareness that you do not walk an easy road.

This is more than likely the one person who will see your mission through until the very end as the success of her mission is inextricably tied to the success of yours.

And Create a New Life

7 Enter the Cave of Becoming

Gift: Understanding

Sacred Warrior Medicine: *"Thank you" is the best prayer that anyone could say. I say that one a lot. Thank you, expresses extreme gratitude, humility and understanding. ~Alice Walker*

I cannot explain the horrors of six and a half months of weekly treatments of chemotherapy poison searing through my veins for six to seven hours at a time. This was followed up with my body rejecting the poison through vomiting, bowel movements and six consecutive months of vaginal bleeding so heavy that I was wearing adult diapers all day. I usually refused to leave my home except to return to the hospital for the treatment that, I was told would give me a 50 percent chance of surviving to 2017.

I was terrified of needles only to constantly have to take tests that every day required I face needles both large and small. The first seven months of breast cancer treatment, I had six blood transfusions. I had two surgeries prior to starting chemotherapy because the first port that was placed in my chest did not function properly.

While living through all of this, of course working was impossible. For the entire two years of the harshest physical treatment, I survived financially from the kindness of friends and neighbors within my community, which expanded because of the Internet.

I have family members all across the globe who I have never met. These men and women, sent money so that my mortgage could be negotiated to stay in the foreclosure process and not be auctioned off.

During this time, letters were written to creditors and I was accompanied to the social services office so that I could receive food assistance from the state of Maryland.

For much of my adult life, I had lived very close to the theoretical education I'd received from reading Robert Kiyosake's books. I had years earlier began paying myself in *real money (gold and silver bullions)*, which I was able to cash in and stay afloat.

Financial self-care before an emergency strikes is critical. It is imperative that you expand your skillset and develop, at the very least, a side gig that is not dependent on your physical or even mental labor to generate a passive, sustainable monthly income for you. I had gotten close, but at the time of my diagnosis, I had yet to master this.

One of the biggest life lessons that I was taught during my days in training at the Inner Visions Institute for Spiritual Development came to life for me during my two years in the Cave of Becoming: Your presence is enough.

Who you are as you find yourself in the Cave of Becoming is valuable. Normally the story we tell ourselves about ourselves when we are in the part of transforming is that we offer nothing of value to our community. *Nothing can be further from the truth.*

The value you bring, especially if you are able and willing to be transparent about your process, is that you allow people to see what the work of metamorphosis looks like. You offer a glimpse into the work that is healing and that for some will alleviate fear and resistance to the healing process in general.

This lesson absolutely amazed me, and to be quite honest, amazes me still to this day. While in the cave, I did what I could: I turned on my video camera and I began telling my story. I shared on a consistent and regular basis, on video, what I was learning about life.

You can still find all of the videos I made in 2012 and 2013 on my YouTube Channel, PathOfSacredWarrior. People from all over the world sent financial contributions to me as I opened up and shared my process. It was in this way that I learned the important lesson that I want to make sure you get today: the fact that you are alive is valuable, you are enough.

When you make the conscious effort to organize what you've learned in your life and present it to the world in a way that they can take the information in, digest it, repurpose it and apply the lessons to their life, *you have created value in the marketplace and people will compensate you for that.* As you will see, this lesson proved invaluable to me later.

I believe that the people from around the globe who were touched by the openness of my healing process became aware that they were getting their own healing, maybe in understanding, in compassion or in learning to honor life and its beautifully messy process.

I don't know who received what exactly. However, I do know that people were more than willing to support the tribal process of healing with the contributions of time, talent, money and the expenditure of personal energy and their presence.

Lesson of Blue Belt: Set a Destination and Go!

Pick a path and move forward. At this rank, you learn that your vision is constantly moving in an effort to seduce you into the adventure of expansion and forward movement. Go toward it.

Hero-in-Training, you have at last come to the Cave of Becoming, a dangerous place, a place where you must become small, sleep more and often go deep underground in your psyche because, Courageous One, this is where the object of your vision quest is hidden.

Hero-in-Training, you have been prepared for this long descent into the most dark, dank innermost cave, an underworld, the void. This is a place where there is nothing and somehow you instinctively know that the greatest potential in your life is here and the only way to receive that infinite potentiality is to dive into this deep, dark hole, alone. You know that access to literally everything is in this place of great trial.

Do not underestimate this place; the danger you sense is very real. You might be forced to enter the cave initially through your mind. You have already taken the deep dive and it is here that your mind begins to play tricks on you, you may begin to doubt your abilities.

I implore you Hero, do not be afraid to face the feelings of being alone and the darkness within so that you can face the darkness outside yourself. Understand that ultimately you enter the world alone. You must take your first breath with the strength and courage of a baby and ultimately, you alone will have to take your last breath with the strength, courage and wisdom of a Hero.

Facing death was the most lonely and difficult thing I have ever done. It will be the most difficult thing all human beings do, even though we all know that there is no escaping death. So, I chose to lean into a relationship with the void, with darkness and with the energy of death. I chose to have a dialogue with death.

Remember that it is inside the dark, dangerous chamber where you will find the elixir that you and your community needs, which is your life's purpose.

You will be reborn physically, emotionally or spiritually because of your ability to face and overcome this trial. Through this experience, Hero-in-Training, you undergo a complete metamorphosis from the inside out. You in no way can live through the depth of this experience and come out of the cave even remotely the same.

What you make it through, must serve you. You will pick up new skills and tools and will become adept in areas you could not even imagine prior to this descent. You will serve the uncharted terrain, tend it, conquer it and ultimately you will tame it. Your reward is that what you live through, energetically bows down and serves you all of the remaining days of your life.

8: Ordeal, Death & Rebirth

Gift: Willpower

Sacred Warrior Medicine: *"With but few exceptions, it is always the underdog who wins through sheer willpower."~Johnny Weissmuller*

July 17, 2012
7 a.m.

I wake up knowing that this is the day I have been preparing for. All of the chemotherapy, all of the tests and transfusions, the vomiting, the hospitalization, the brain fog, the complete lack of immunity and total loss of hair from every conceivable part of my body was for one reason.

Going to the infusion clinic left me feeling like I had climbed into the boxing ring with a silverback gorilla every seven days, was pummeled within an inch of my life and was left hanging in the balance for days.

All of that was to shrink the tumor as much as possible so that I could surrender my body to the knife for a double mastectomy surgery.

I walked into the operating room and climbed onto the table. Would I ever see my partner, Aina-Nia, and good friend, Reverend Anthony again? They walked me to a thick white line, I kissed them both and the rest I had to do on my own.

I had filled out the paperwork for what I wanted done should I die on the operating table. I watched the technicians swarm around the room like bees. A nurse strapped my arms to the table and as she placed the mask over my nose and mouth, I breathed and a tear ran down the outside of my eyes. 4, 3, 2 ....

A little after 5 a.m., I felt the gentle hand of my oncology nurse navigator nudging me to wake up. "Welcome back, Alicia," she said. "We need to get you into the bathroom so that you can try to move your bowels."

I looked at her like she had three heads and looked down at my own chest, which was wrapped tightly in bandages and was almost flat. After the eight-and-a-half hours of surgery, breasts were gone and my head was spinning. How in the world did she expect me to walk across the floor when everything hurt? I was pissed. I felt weak. I needed to vomit. I was bald and cold and terribly afraid. I was afraid of my body, I was afraid to look at the disfigurement.

I knew I would live and be strong again somehow, someday. I shimmied to the edge of the bed using just my behind. (I could not use my arms since they had removed 35 lymph nodes from my right arm in addition to both breasts).

I cussed and cried in anger that fueled my resolve to live. I knew I still had another four years of treatments ahead of me and who knew what else. But I had woken up dammit and so I knew I would fight to continue living. I had the audacity to look death in its face and live!

Alicia was a distant memory.

It was at this juncture that I knew everything about me had changed. Subira Folami stepped to the forefront of my life that morning and took over living.

Lesson of Blue Belt: Set a Destination and Go!

Pick a path and move forward. At this rank, you learn that your vision is constantly moving in an effort to seduce you into the adventure of expansion and forward movement. Go toward it.

You have made it to the half waypoint of your odyssey. You'll know it because this is the place where you find yourself asking, "Can things get any worse?" and they do! You are smack dab in the middle of the Hero's Journey and this is the moment when you have to look death or at least a situation that feels like death, square in the eye.

Here is the good news, Hero-in-Training: to keep moving forward in your life, to advance rather than become stuck in fear, to transform into a new person, you must come to a kind of death, and out of the moment of death you are transformed into a new life.

This abyss serves you by taking you through the final separation from your Ordinary World and from the person you were in that land. By entering this stage of the Hero's Journey, you demonstrate to your life's purpose that you are willing to live through even a catastrophic personal metamorphosis so that you become who you need to be to align with your life purpose and vision.

You prove that you are completely committed to become the person who is able to serve humanity in a way that will be revealed to you in the future.

You are willing to take this last plunge into the unknown so that you can release the false pretense and the personality trappings that society handed you and reinforced throughout your life.

You now know that the life you are living does not belong to you. So you do the noble thing and stop living a life that is not authentically you.

It is true that you may well feel put upon by life at first. You will feel as though you are being thrust into this stage by circumstances and forced to make difficult choices.

That is how all Sacred Warriors feel when suddenly confronting death or dire situations. And then one day, a dawning happens and you realize that you were living a life of quiet desperation, the energy that your life had been floating on was a low, silent hum of "I want out of all this!" Well, this is the way out of the trappings of a life that has been holding you prisoner. This journey, this process, has come to free you.

And at the same time, you are always at choice. You always have the freedom to decide how you will face or refuse to face, the situation that is threatening to your psychological, emotional, mental and at times physical well-being. You will discover that this pivotal point is your moment of grace.

This is the point when you realize that the value you've been clinging to will only lead to your physical detriment, and that you can instead choose to embrace your life's purpose and vision and this leads to an improved life for you and everyone who is in your life.

In your life's journey, you will face many "deaths to the self." So ask yourself, are you dancing around the perimeter of an abyss in your Hero's Journey? What choices do you see before you? Do you have mentors in your life who can support you in identifying your blind spots?

Here your life hits rock bottom in a direct confrontation with the greatest fear that has been running your life. You will have to face the possibility of death and in one way or another. You will be brought to your edge in a battle with a Worthy Opponent.

For some time, you will have to sit in suspense and cosmic tension. At worst, you will not know if you will live or at best, die. You will have to face this as a thought. However, your physical life will not truly be at risk.

Needless to say, this is a critical moment in your journey. You must die or appear to die for the process of regeneration and rebirth to occur through you. It's a major source of the mysticism of your heroic journey.

The world will appear brand new to you. Your body will feel differently to you. Food tastes differently. You may find that your intuition has heightened and you may have a childlike feeling of elation and exhilaration.

This is where you must exert your willpower. You must will yourself to overcome the seemingly insurmountable. You must feel the fear and allow yourself to transform. Allow everything that is no longer you to gently fall away, be cut out, burned off and exhaled back into the nothingness from which it came. By doing so, you allow the old you to be transformed and return to life, prayerfully to serve another.

Let yourself go so that the fears can no longer hold you down, hold you back, lie to you or even coerce you into lying to others about who you are.

At this point, you will no longer accept castles built in the sand, because you are afraid of the work required to build into solid ground. Yes, I say into the ground, because you will need to will yourself to do some digging to locate the authentic you. And when you find her (or him), trust me, she or he will never let you go. You will have emerged regal and triumphant.

9 Reward, Seize the Sword

Gift: Order

Sacred Warrior Medicine: "I go to nature to be soothed and healed, and to have my senses put in order."~*John Burroughs*

Lesson of Blue Belt: Set a Destination and Go!

Pick a path and move forward. At this rank, you learn that your vision is constantly moving in an effort to seduce you into the adventure of expansion and forward movement. Go toward it.

You are alive. You have survived. You overcame your deepest fear(s). Believe me, you have been forever transformed, been made into a completely new BEing.

One of the rewards of making it through this process is the gift of breathing with ease. It is at this point on your journey that you receive reprieve from the relentless pace that you have been experiencing. This is where, without a doubt, you know you have reached a new turning point in your rite of passage.

After defeating the enemy, surviving death and finally overcoming his greatest personal challenge, the Hero is ultimately transformed into a new state, emerging from battle as a stronger person and often with a prize.

The Reward may come in many forms: an object of great importance or power, a secret, greater knowledge or insight, or even reconciliation with a loved one or ally. Whatever the treasure, which may well facilitate his return to the Ordinary World, the Hero must quickly put celebrations aside and prepare for the last leg of his journey.

The Hero takes possession of the treasure won by facing death. There may be a celebration, but there is also danger of losing the treasure again.

10 The Road Back Home

Gift: Zeal

Sacred Warrior Medicine: *"I have an almost religious zeal ... not for technology per se, but for the Internet which is for me, likened to the nervous system of mother Earth, which I see as a living creature, linking up."~Sensei Subira (Adapted from a Dan Millman quote)*

June 7, 2012
3:38 p.m.
Michael's Craft store

Crystal was walking through Michael's with me as I looked at toys to bring home as a gift for myself to celebrate! Earlier that week I completed the sixth month of chemotherapy. I remember feeling like I needed a lion, a phoenix and a dragon. And then my cellphone rang.

I had been vaginally hemorrhaging for the entire 6.5 months of chemotherapy. It was so bad that I was unable to leave my home for more than a few hours at a time and prior to every chemo treatment, I received a blood transfusion.

Standing in the middle of the toy aisle, my oncology surgeon called me to tell me that my numbers were too low to do the surgery and that if she put me on the table now, I was not going to be strong enough to come through it.

"What does that mean ... What are you telling me?" I asked her. Dr. Fernandez replied that I would need one more blood transfusion, one more chemotherapy treatment and they would need to start me on a new, stronger drug that would force me into menopause.

I had been getting a different hormone suppressant for the previous six months, but it hadn't stopped the bleeding. I went into the infusion clinic and received all of the treatments she laid out in hopes that we could move forward and cut out what was left of the CANcer.

After the double mastectomy, I was given a 30-day reprieve followed by 35 days of intense radiation therapy. This was done to burn any remaining CANcer cells that chemotherapy drugs did not poison and any that were not cut out during the surgery.

Every day for 35 days I laid down on a table in a room. It was not until the technicians had left the room, that the 12-inch-thick impenetrable metal door was closed and radiation was pointed and shot through my chest. I was on The Road Back Home, but this was *not* the last major challenge I had to overcome.

Lesson of Purple Belt: Great Purpose Summons Great Energy

You were born on purpose, with a purpose and it is that very purpose, which will fill you with the energy to accomplish whatever challenges you encounter.

Hero, this is the place on your journey where you will get one last opportunity to reconcile with the parent, the gods or the hostile forces with whom you may have an incomplete emotional business.

You can leave this layer of hurt on the Hero's Journey and allow yourself to be free of the burdens of who you were before setting out on this journey.

If you do this, I guarantee you that when you meet with the people and situations from your past, when you return to the places of old, you will know that you are free because you actually left it all there and the release allowed you to become a new BEing.

You will, for the first time in your life, experience a truth, authenticity and a freedom that no words I can write here, can even come close to explaining.

You will realize that the Hero's Journey must eventually be left behind, but there are still dangers, temptations, and tests ahead. However, you will also know that the person you have transformed into is equipped to navigate anything that The Ordinary World brings your way.

You must decide whether you are going to begin the journey to return home to the Ordinary World or remain on the journey. This is where you learn that you are always at choice. During your Hero's Journey you also came to know that although this Special World has its charms, you might not want to stay there permanently.

You went there to transform, to grow, to unleash more of who you truly are by learning to tap into and wield your gifts and powers. Ultimately, you went there to bring back the gift of your authenticity and the medicine that only you could locate and carry back to your community.

This is another demarcation on the timeline of your psychological, emotional, physical and spiritual development.

Now is the turning point where you must choose to rededicate yourself to the adventure of living in alignment with the truth of who you are all the time; *especially upon arriving back home.*

The beautiful thing about this place is that as long as you return fully embodying your "New New," as they call it in chemo, the people in the Ordinary World will adjust. If, however, you vacillate due to your own discomfort, others in your world will be unsure about who you are and the easiest thing to do is to revert back to the *you that they are used to.* The problem is you will know that you are no longer that person.

The Road Back Home is not paved with gold. What you must always remember is that the Hero's Journey, by definition, is a life full setbacks, switchbacks and obstacles and some will last a few minutes while others go on like an elaborate string of ordeals.

The main purpose of it all is to acknowledge the Hero's resolve to finish your journey, to expand in your understanding of both the Ordinary and Special Worlds. To take what you have learned and all that you have received and prepare yourself for the new goal, for further adventure and, to each time, return home with stronger medicine that supports humanity and more specifically, the community that you have a sacred agreement to serve.

Sometimes, there are consequences that the Hero must face as a result of the previous stage. You may still have to confront your Worthy Opponent before you can begin your trek home.

Keep in mind, that there will be times you go out on a Hero's Journey and the goal isn't only to get home, but to find new, greater treasures within. Sometimes, the Road Back Home is simply about how you leave a place or situation and then, if and how you return.

There will be journeys that are void of pomp and circumstance, the test is simply to show you and your community what grace or chaos can look like and both of these are valuable demonstrations to live and learn through.

This stage in your development is about understanding that you have indeed transformed to the point that you can return home, anchored in the new BEing that you have become since embarking upon the journey.

This is when you discover that old familiar ways are no longer effective. You learn that you will need to call upon the new information that you have learned or been granted. So, find a new way and use your new tools so that you can carry yourself over the line of completion of the adventure at hand.

There is one final test on the journey.

11 The Resurrection

Gift: Release

Sacred Warrior Medicine: *"Life isn't about finding yourself. Life is about creating yourself."~George Bernard Shaw*

December 28, 2012
The Phone Call

All I knew at that point was that for things in our relationship to stay the same, things needed to change. I had finally built up the courage to request from my partner that we begin looking at changing things in the relationship, or I knew I would have to leave.
I had only imagined that I would be told that of course we would work on the relationship. But what I heard streaming through the other end of the phone were these words, "No. I cannot give you what you need."

My heart absolutely broke. How could we come this far? Had she wanted to leave the entire time, but waited until she thought I was strong enough to handle her leaving? Was she hoping *I* would leave the relationship? So many questions flooded my mind, so much hurt.

I thought surely I would die. Somehow, I had to figure my way through this pain, but I sincerely thought I could take no more. After releasing everything that this journey had required of me, I didn't know that I could let go of the love of my life.

However, I had to. I learned my own strength. I dug deeper into myself, I pulled on every skill, tool, friendship, song, breath. I attended every yoga class and martial arts class. I sang and danced and eventually laughed my way into resurrection.

I had misunderstood. If I was going to live, it was I who needed to transform. Releasing this relationship was the last and the most painful death I needed to live through to be resurrected. So, I became a new person.

2014

Each month in 2014, another woman I knew and loved died from CANcer. Usually, the Worthy Opponent dies or are defeated, but sometimes, the Hero dies.

There were a total of 14 fallen warriors in my life between January and December 2014.

Instead of living on mortally, these Sheroes are resurrected in the sense that they will live on in the memory of those who continue to live in the physical.

All of these women fought unimaginably difficult battles and the most loving decision they could make for themselves was to release the body. I believe that these women of valor signed a sacred agreement in which they could be more powerfully effective in the ancestral realm. From this place, they act as Guide and Mentor. And for this Sacred Knowledge, I am so grateful.

Lesson of Brown Belt: Exhale First, Then Create

Exhale first, then create. Here you learn to master the conscious use of your breath, doing this gives you access to the power to re-create yourself over and over again.

In a sense, this is your final exam Beloved Hero. The symbolic part of this death and resurrection has everything to do with solidifying your transformation. It is here where you must prove for the final time that you truly have changed and that when you walk back into the Ordinary World, you will do it as a new woman or man.

You will be able to more compassionately respond to people and to life. You will be both tender and strong, resilient and steadfast. You are now both follower and more importantly, you re-enter the world as a capable leader who serves from the heart.

You had to transform to deal with the Special World, and now you pull together the good parts of that transformation with the good parts of the Ordinary World self to create a new self.

This phase of transformation is about dying to everything that held you back or down in the Ordinary World, so that you can experience a higher expression of yourself, of possibility, of life and of love. Let go so that you can rise up, Sacred Warrior!

My grandmother, who our family lovingly calls, "Mommy 2," had a saying when she was alive that still rings in my head, "Everybody wants to go to heaven, but nobody wants to die."

That phrase took on special meaning at the end of 2012.The Resurrection phase of the Hero's life cycle is hard work, mainly because, as you can see, it is *not* a one-time event.

During the transformation process, you lived through several phases, and each can be thought of as a cycle within the transformation process. And every phase has its own life, death and resurrection.

As long as you are alive, you will repeatedly return from the dead. This is actually what it means to live and grow. Your life will repeatedly give you, The Hero, another opportunity to "Begin Again" using all lessons learned on the journey. You will be transformed into a new Being with new insights and this continually elevates your instincts, awareness and expands your consciousness.

One of the experiences that you, The Hero, must become comfortable with, is release. By definition, being a Hero means you will always be somewhere in the process of initiation. You must be taken right to the edge of death, clearly sharpen your life skills and this is how you best serve humanity: *by becoming adept in the art of living*.

Your Resurrection will not always be life shattering. Some of them will be more like a gentle cresting of a wave of emotion. Many of your journeys will be experienced on the mental plane, or only physically.

Other times the Journey will ask that your behavior, feelings or beliefs about certain things transform. Either way, this stage in your journey is signaled by a feeling of catharsis, a purifying emotional release. This purification must occur so that you can move forward with a light heart and without emotional or psychological encumbrances.

Psychologically you can expect anxiety or depression to be released from you by bringing unconscious material to the surface for you to confront. In the spiritual arena, we call this a healing crisis. At this point, the Hero has reached the highest point of awareness.

Because catharsis works best through a physical expression of emotions such as laughter or tears, expect many. From 2012 to 2014, I literally cried every day. I hadn't previously known that my energetic and emotional bodies could process this much continual grief and release.

I certainly would not have begun to imagine that I could actually live through all of that in addition to the added layers of unrelenting, sheer physical pain for the same time period.

Sacred Warrior, you are stronger than you can ever imagine. However, you will only come to know your own strength by being taken to the edge of the ledge and summoning the courage to keep breathing.

You facing the Resurrection will simultaneously be your most dangerous meeting with death and the final push to make your way into the world anew.

This final life-and-death challenge proves to your psyche what your spirit and consciousness already knows deep down, that you have maintained and can apply all that you have brought back to the Ordinary World.

As painful as your emergence from the land of the dead may feel, the ultimate result will be your complete freedom. You will be reborn and transformed with the attributes of your ordinary self who is now enhanced due to the lessons and insights from the characters that you traveled with along the road.

Understand that the transformation is for much more than the Hero's life. Other people's lives or entire global communities may be at stake. You, the Hero, must now prove that you are willing, ready and able to accept this sacrifice for the benefit of those operating in the Ordinary World and who are counting on you to make it back to them with the wisdom, insights and medicine that only you can carry.

The Hero's Journey will always give you traveling companions, and other allies may come to the last-minute rescue to lend assistance, but in the end it is you who must undergo a final purging and purification before returning to the Ordinary World. It is you alone who must rise up.

And Create a New Life

12 Return With The Elixir

Gift: Life

Sacred Warrior Medicine: *"I turned to music originally because of my past and needing a release or an outlet to get out anger or frustration or hurt."*
~Christina Aguilera

Tuesday
July 5, 2016
5:30 a.m.

I turn over in my sleep and this wakes me up. I reach over and grab the glass of water on my nightstand and pop a Tamoxifen in my mouth. Every morning I take this pill, which promises to block breast CANcer from returning.

I make my way upstairs to my prayer and meditation room, and spend some time taking in the sound of silence and the heavy yet clean aroma of incense. Once I feel anchored inside, I come downstairs and begin my day with a piping hot cup of dandelion coffee.

Opening my computer, my mind searches for topics

that I feel led to speak about during my daily Facebook livestream that broadcasts at noon. I also review materials to share with the group of spiritual entrepreneurs that I teach weekly.

Just as I am completing my broadcast outline, the phone rings and it is a woman I met three years ago. We weren't friends, per se, however, she called to tell me that her young child is in the hospital fighting for his life and she remembered the story of my journey and my fight. She tells me she wants my help telling her story of the transformation that she and her son are traveling through together. I feel humbled and honored. I tell her, "Yes, I will support you."

My heart opens wide knowing that it is for this moment, that I faced and conquered breast CANcer. Days later, I facilitate an interview with her so that she can share what is on her heart and she begins the process of writing her book. The first assignment I give her is to make a video as often as she can as well as journal so that she can capture these very precious moments during this very challenging time.

My life has changed completely since I first felt the lump in my breast. Today I am living the vision of the life that I held in my heart and mind during those painful, lonely, dark days and nights.

In the process of my own healing, I started a company teaching yoga and martial arts (a vision that I have had for 25 years). I earned my second-degree black belt in American Kenpo in 2016. Today through my company, www.SenseiSubira.com, I now support healers, light workers, spiritual entrepreneurs of all kinds and aspiring authors to use the power of their stories to create sustainable, joy-filled businesses that align with their hearts and life purposes.

Lesson of Black Belt: Go As Far As You Can and Then One Step Further

When you think that you have gone as far as you can, you find that inside of you is a reserve of everything you need to go a little further, and this "little bit," is what makes you the Hero.

This is the final stage of the Hero's journey in which he returns home to his Ordinary World, a changed person. Sacred Warrior, you are a BEing in search of yourself. Many times the best way to discover yourself is to lose yourself.

Just as shedding your old self to gain entry into the Special World was a necessary part of your initiation, you must again be willing to shed the self that has been on this grand adventure, the one who has learned so much.

One of my spiritual teachers, a wise man named Babalawo Obaniyi, has repeated this Yoruba proverb to me many times, "Stoop To Conquer." It means that with self-mastery you need to become increasingly humble to be able to have a positive influence on others.

Once your transformation is complete, Hero, your assignment is to return to the Ordinary World with the elixir, a great treasure or a new understanding to share. Your new self will reflect the best parts of your old self while simultaneously incorporating the lessons you have integrated into your BEingness through the wisdom, lessons and insights that you received during your Hero's Journey. To learn something in the

Special World is one thing. To bring the knowledge home and apply it is another thing entirely.

The elixir that each Hero must return home with is different. It usually will not be a tangible gift. The community that I serve was in need of something only I carried and the same is true for you. Heros are the recipients who need it most and who receive the elixir first. As I have said earlier, it is actually a medicine that is opened up in or through you and only you can bring this medicine home.

For some Sacred Warriors the elixir will be Love, for others Wisdom, Freedom, Compassion, Peace or the knowledge that the Special World exists and can be overcome.

Some Heros are seeking the medicine of Life. Either way, unless an elixir is brought back from the ordeal in the innermost cave, you, The Hero, are doomed to repeat the adventure.

Love, Vision and Purpose are three of the most powerful and popular of elixirs and they are the ones I now carry and share with the world.

If you have made it to this point, the complex act of re-entry into the Ordinary World closes a circle, bringing deep healing, wellness and wholeness to the Ordinary World.

The gift of your returning with the elixir means that your very presence has earned you the right to implement change in daily life and use the wisdom of the adventure to offer healing to a wounded world.

Before crossing the threshold that brings you back, you must show appreciation and say farewell to the allies that worked with you, nursed you, laughed, cried and traveled with you. They may or may not have known that at some point you would have to move forward without them, because as the Hero, you must always return home.

Once you cross over into the Ordinary World, you are

immediately made aware that your perceptions of the people in your life have changed. Your senses are heightened, your compassion, strength and courage are much more far-reaching than before you left.

You may notice that you no longer sweat the small stuff and you realize that *most of it is small stuff.* You are laser clear on why you are alive and that invigorates most and frightens others. You are completely comfortable with both emotions.

You may discover that your return brings fresh hope to those allies you left behind, a direct solution to their problems or perhaps a new perspective for everyone in your world, past, present or future to consider.

The final reward that you can look forward to may be literal or metaphoric. It could be a cause for celebration, self-realization or an end to strife. Whatever it is it surely represents three things: transformation, success and proof that you did in fact go away and were re-configured while on the journey.

The other key point to know is that since transformation happens in community, your return home brings resolution for the people in your life. Those who doubted you may find themselves ostracized, those who worked against you during this challenging time will now face challenges of their own and those who supported you, Life will greatly reward.

Ultimately you will go back to where you began, however, neither you nor home will ever be the same again. Some element of the elixir has been grafted to you that has the power to transform the world as you were transformed.

This is your destiny, Sacred Warrior, and the world needs you to go through the transformative experience so that you remember that you are the Hero that you've been looking for. By accepting this knowledge, you will nurture a deep knowing that you came to conquer and offer new expressions of hope, healing and power. So that you can find your voice and begin to use it to ROOOAAARRR!

About the Author

Sensei Subira is a speaker, minister, life coach, teacher, martial artist, yoga teacher and author, who believes that our most painful life experiences can serve as a catalyst for transformation. She believes that the powerful process of confronting pain can heal us, our tribe and by extension the world. She is described as, "The Demonstration of Divine Transformation!"

Sensei Subira has an intimate knowledge of the transformative power of a life disrupted. While navigating treatment of stage 3 breast CANcer during 2012 and 2013, Sensei Subira began serving thousands of men and women through her YOUnique life message of Transformation via her daily YouTube videos and Facebook posts where she transparently shared her journey. She organically grew a social media tribe by simply being herself and sharing what she was learning on the journey.

As her body healed, she became more in tune with her passion and purpose—to guide a tribe of Enlightened Entrepreneurs through the process of discovering how their stories of transformational life experiences will heal them and align them with their tribe so that they can serve them more deeply.

Using as her foundation her most powerful life lessons, Sensei Subira coaches, teaches and inspires through her innovative, balanced and cutting-edge approach to connecting with, nurturing and serving her tribe both online and in person.

 Sensei Subira believes that the key to wellness lies in moving with the call to transform and that wholeness and healing lies in understanding M.O.N.E.Y. (My Own Natural Energy Yield), which she defines as: "Your ability to tap into, harness and direct with total personal authority, your YOUnique life experiences shared with your tribe transparently, innate gifts, patterns, skills, as well as simple tools used to uplift the planet."

This contributing author of the international best-selling anthology, *Living Without Limitations-30 Mentors To Rock Your World,* uses as her foundation, Universal Laws and Principles. Sensei Subira holds a second-degree black belt in American Kenpo Martial Arts, a red belt in Budokon Martial Arts & Yoga and is a Reiki Master Teacher.

She was ordained at the Inner Visions Institute for Spiritual Development under the distinguished tutelage of Master Life Coach and Spiritual teacher, world renowned speaker, best-selling author, radio and television personality, Iyanla Vanzant.

Subira Speaks

My purpose is to teach Enlightened Entrepreneurs like you, how to use your powerful stories of personal transformation to create sustainable, passive income so that you are free to live aligned with your purpose.

Here are the topics I love to speak about:

*You Are The Hero You've Been Waiting For
*Dis-Ease as the Doorway to Creating The Life of Your Dreams
*Storytelling as a Spiritual and Business Practice
*Gold as Your Family's Financial Insurance

Contact Subira at:
434.878.2472
www.SenseiSubira.com/VIP

Made in the USA
Columbia, SC
20 August 2017